D0568960

Pumpkins and Squash

Pumpkins and Squash

BY KATHLEEN DESMOND STANG

PHOTOGRAPHS BY LAURIE FRANKEL

CHRONICLE BOOKS
SAN FRANCISCO

"We have pumpkins at morning, pumpkins at noon.
If it were not for pumpkins we should be undoon."

Anonymous
(Seventeenth-Century New England)

TO MY SIBLINGS,
MARGARET, EILEEN, JERRY, AND PATRICIA,
AND TO BOB, SQUASH LOVERS ALL.

ACKNOWLEDGMENTS
Special thanks to all who helped, especially to Leslie Jonath, to Susan Derecskey, and to Dr. James R. Baggett for his help with the Glossary.

This edition published in 2005 by Chronicle Books LLC for Williams-Sonoma, Inc.

ISBN 0-8118-4993-7

Manufactured in China
Design by Laurie Frankel
Food Styling by Robyn Valerik
Prop styling by Alessandra Mortola
10 9 8 7 6 5 4 3 2 1

Chronicle Books LLC
85 Second Street
San Francisco, California 94105
www.chroniclebooks.com

Page 2: Classic Pumpkin-Pecan Pie, page 66.

Contents

About pumpkins and squash

If asked to name my favorite vegetable, I'd pick a squash any time.

Squashes come in all shapes, sizes, and colors, from the classic, straightneck butternut squash, to the legendary Blue Hubbard, to rich green summer zucchini, to delicious mini-pumpkins. This nutritious vegetable lends itself to a nearly endless list of recipes that will tempt any palate. Squashes are easy to find, easy to cook, and especially easy to eat.

In summer, I search for the tastiest yellow crookneck squash. An old-fashioned variety, it is at its best when picked and, within the hour, sautéed or grilled, and sprinkled with a little fresh thyme.

Although sometimes classified as a fruit, pumpkins commonly serve as vegetables in cooking and can be used in recipes that call for squash or even sweet potatoes. On a blustery fall afternoon I delight in plump pumpkins piled high at farm stands, as well as the little sugar pumpkin, the kind to bake with maple syrup as our ancestors might have done.

In winter, I'd have to vote for the creamy, rich flavor and colorful shape of the turban squash. This green-, gold-, and orange-splotched squash makes a spectacular fall centerpiece. That is, until it is turned into a steaming soup that fills the house with its fragrance.

Come each new spring season, I delight in experimenting with new, flavorful uses for this king of vegetables. Rich in flavor and nutrients, most squashes, including pumpkins, can easily be stored for months—until the mood strikes to turn your squash or pumpkin into bread, soups, stews, puddings, pies, or ice cream!

SUMMER VERSUS WINTER SQUASH

Squashes and pumpkins, along with cucumbers and melons, are part of the vast gourd family known as Cucurbitaceae.

Most squashes, including pumpkins, are in the genus Cucurbita, which is generally subdivided into two groups: tender-skinned summer squash and hard-shelled winter squash.

The summer squashes are identified by their thin skin and mild flavor. The entire squash is edible, including the blossom, skin, and seeds. Examples include the scallop-edged pattypan, bright yellow Sunburst, and the prolific zucchini. This group, commonly referred to as summer squash, is picked immature, while the skin is still tender and the flavor delicate. In general, the different types can be used interchangeably in recipes. The peak season for summer squash is July through September.

Winter squash, on the other hand, is allowed to ripen to maturity. The shell hardens to protect the meaty interior and may no longer be edible. The range of winter squash includes smooth-skinned butternut with its exceptional nutty flavor and bright orange meat; elongated, green-striped Delicata; and the tiny, edible mini-pumpkins, such as Jack-Be-Little and Munchkin.

Pumpkins, those orange globes of autumn, are famous for Halloween jack-o'-lanterns and holiday pumpkin pie. But are pumpkins really any different from other squashes? Actually, no. Be they large for carving or small for baking, all pumpkins are members of the winter squash group.

Unlike tender summer squashes, which can be eaten raw, winter squashes must be cooked to make them palatable as well as to bring out their characteristic flavors, whether mild or bold, nutlike or sweet. The texture of winter squash ranges from coarse or fibrous to smooth and creamy. Although there are many sizes and shapes, most of the different varieties of winter squash can be used interchangeably.

Winter squash is generally planted in summer and harvested

in the fall. The squash stores well in a cool, dark, dry place for several months. The peak buying season is September through February, though some varieties, with proper storage, keep well for a year.

The yellow-skinned spaghetti squash fits somewhere between summer squash and winter squash. When cooked, the meat turns into flavorful, golden, spaghetti-like strands that are easy to scrape out of the shell with a fork. Its buying season is August through February.

For more information, see the glossary of squash varieties on page 74.

CHOOSING AND STORING SQUASH

Select squash carefully for maximum flavor and nutrients.

When purchasing summer squash, look for firm specimens heavy for their size. Avoid any that are bruised or moldy. Summer squash will last only three or four days. Keep it, unwashed, in an unsealed bag in the crisper drawer of the refrigerator.

Winter squash, on the other hand, will last for months if properly handled. Choose specimens that are firm and heavy for their size. Avoid any with cracks or signs of decay.

For cooking and baking, select small to medium pie pumpkins, such as New England Pie, Small Sugar, Baby Pam, or Mystic pumpkins. Their sweet, deep-orange flesh characteristically has a smooth, stringless texture. Flavorful, stringless, and easy to peel and prepare, crookneck pumpkins are a great choice anytime.

Often, the best pumpkins for carving into jack-o'-lanterns will have tough skins that may be difficult to peel, as well as stringy, tasteless flesh. You can compromise by seeking out newer varieties of ornamental pumpkins that offer both winsome flavor and decorative appeal, such as Jarradale, Fairytale, or Lumina pumpkins.

Store hard-shelled squash in a well-ventilated, dark, cool, dry place for up to six months. Check occasionally, particularly on the underside, to be sure no soft spots have developed.

Large squash, such as Hubbard, are often sold in pieces. These can be loosely wrapped and refrigerated for several days.

For longer storage, any of the hard-shelled varieties, including the small pumpkins, can be steamed, baked, or microwaved (see Cooked Spaghetti Squash, page 22) until tender, then puréed. Cover tightly and freeze for up to six months.

COOKING WITH SQUASH

The two groups of squash—thin-skinned summer squash and hard-shelled winter squash—are handled in entirely different ways in the kitchen.

To prepare summer squash, rinse the squash just before cooking, but do not peel it unless the squash is overgrown and the skin is tough. In that case, you may need to discard the seeds too. Cut off and discard the ends. Slice, dice, or julienne the squash, or leave it whole.

The many varieties of thin-skinned squash can be treated basically in the same way. Summer squash requires little or no cooking. Sliced raw squash is a good addition to crudités or on a relish tray.

Stir-frying, steaming, and microwaving are ideal cooking methods for these tender, mild squashes. Slice or dice the squash and stir-fry in a little olive or vegetable oil until crisp-tender. Steam whole or sliced squash on a rack over boiling water, being careful not to overcook. Or microwave sliced squash tossed with minced herbs and black pepper for a fat-free vegetable dish.

Allow about four to eight ounces of summer squash per serving.

To prepare winter squash, rinse the squash and, depending on the size and shape, cut it in half or cut off the top to form a container for stuffing. Scoop out and discard the seeds and fibers (unless you are saving the seeds to toast). Cut large squash, such as Hubbard and banana, into serving pieces.

Some squash shells are so tough they may require an ax or a hacksaw to cut them. Another option is to poke a few holes in the squash and then bake or microwave it to soften before cutting.

In general, all the hard-shelled squash can be cooked and used in the same way. For best results, bake winter squash in a conventional oven or microwave oven. Bake, cut side down, on a baking sheet, at 350 to 375° F until fork tender. Or microwave in a covered dish, cut side down, with a few spoonfuls of water at "high" (100%) for seven to ten minutes per pound. Then let stand a few minutes to finish cooking. This method may not be as flavorful as baking, but it certainly is convenient. Boiling and steaming are less successful, because the squash tends to absorb the moisture and become watery.

Season winter squash with sweet, fruity, and spicy flavors, such as maple syrup or brown sugar, diced apples or shredded orange peel, cinnamon or ginger. Or go the savory route with herbs, chilies, or just salt and freshly ground pepper.

Plan on at least six to eight ounces of winter squash per person.

You can interchange pumpkins and most types of winter squash in recipes. The lightly ribbed white Lumina pumpkins have bright orange flesh that's great for cooking and baking, as does the thick and tender and wonderfully flavorful Fairytale pumpkin.

Place round pumpkins on a piece of butcher paper or a newspaper. Cut downward into the pumpkin to slice in half, then scoop out the seeds and fibers. Cut into sections, wash, and remove the orange skin with a paring knife. Cook or bake in a conventional oven or microwave, as desired (see pages 22, 34).

Crookneck pumpkins, by far the easiest to cook, should be carefully washed, dried, and cut into 3- to 4-inch pieces, cutting the hollow end that holds the seeds in half and then removing the seeds. Peel, cut into smaller pieces, and cook cut side down in a large saucepan in a small amount of boiling water until tender, 20 to 30 minutes.

Purée the cooked pumpkin in a blender or food processor and refrigerate for up to two days or freeze in an airtight container (see page 34). It is smart to freeze in containers accommodating the amounts needed for your favorite recipes.

A YEAR-ROUND TREAT

Squash is always available. In summer, it may be hard to keep up with the out-of-control zucchini. But soon the fields are dotted with golden pumpkins, poking out from the fading leaves. Even in winter, zucchini and acorn squash are in the supermarket produce bins. And there is always the old reliable, canned pumpkin purée, a pantry standby.

Pumpkin and squash, a year-round treat—for breakfast, lunch, dinner, and dessert!

BREADS AND BREAKFAST

Almond-pumpkin coffee cake wreaths

MAKES 2 WREATHS

1 recipe Two-Way Pumpkin Yeast Dough (page 26)

1 can (8 ounces) almond paste, crumbled

4 tablespoons butter (½ stick) at room temperature

¼ cup (packed) light brown sugar

2 tablespoons all-purpose flour

½ teaspoon ground cinnamon

1 egg yolk, beaten with 1 tablespoon water

¼ cup sliced almonds

Serve one coffee cake hot from the oven. Wrap and freeze the second one for another time.

◆ Divide the dough into 2 equal parts. Cover and let rest for 10 minutes.

◆ Combine the almond paste, butter, brown sugar, flour, and cinnamon in a bowl. Set aside. Roll out 1 piece of dough to a 24-by-9-inch rectangle on a lightly floured surface. Sprinkle with half of the almond paste mixture. From the long side, roll up loosely, jelly-roll fashion. Transfer the roll, seam side down, to a large greased baking sheet and press together ends to form a ring. Using kitchen shears or a sharp knife, make cuts to the inside circle, every ½ inch, three quarters of the way along the outer edge of the ring. Turn the cuts on an angle to expose the filling.

◆ Repeat for the second ring. Cover and let rise in a warm place until puffy, about 30 minutes.

◆ Preheat oven to 350°F. Brush the rings with egg wash and sprinkle with almonds. Brush again with egg wash. Bake for 30 to 35 minutes, or until golden brown. Transfer to a rack.

◆ Serve warm or at room temperature.

Whole wheat zucchini bread

MAKES 1 LOAF

1 large (about 8 ounces) zucchini or other summer squash

1 cup whole wheat flour

¾ cup all-purpose flour

1 teaspoon ground cinnamon

½ teaspoon baking soda

¼ teaspoon baking powder

½ teaspoon salt

¾ cup (packed) brown sugar

½ cup milk

¼ cup vegetable oil

1 large egg, lightly beaten

1 teaspoon grated lemon peel

½ teaspoon vanilla extract

½ cup currants or chopped walnuts

Use zucchini, pattypan, or crookneck, whichever summer squash is the most abundant.

◆ Preheat oven to 350°F. Position the coarse shredding disk in a food processor and shred the zucchini. Set aside. You should have 1 cup.

◆ Combine the whole wheat flour, all-purpose flour, cinnamon, baking soda, baking powder, and salt in a large bowl. Set aside.

◆ Position the knife blade in the food processor. Put the brown sugar, milk, oil, egg, lemon peel, and vanilla in the food processor bowl. Pulse on and off until mixed. Add the shredded zucchini and currants. Pulse on and off until well mixed. Add the flour mixture and pulse on and off just until combined. Spoon into a greased 8½-by-4½-by-2½-inch loaf pan. Bake for 50 to 60 minutes, or until a wooden toothpick inserted near the center comes out clean. Cool in the pan for 10 minutes. Unmold onto a rack to cool thoroughly.

◆ Cut into ½-inch slices to serve.

Halloween jack-o'-lantern breads

This bread is particularly good toasted and spread with orange marmalade.

MAKES 4 BREADS

- I recipe Two-Way Pumpkin Yeast Dough (page 26)
- Currants for decoration
- I egg white, beaten with 2 teaspoons water
- Cinnamon sugar for sprinkling (optional)

◆ Divide the dough into 4 equal parts. Cover and let rest for 5 to 10 minutes.

◆ Use I piece of the dough for each jack-o'-lantern. Pinch off a small knob of dough and shape into a pumpkin stem. Shape the remaining dough into a ball and flatten to make a pumpkin shape about 9-by-7 inches. Place on greased baking sheet and add the stem, so that the two pieces will connect while baking. Make shallow cuts to resemble a pumpkin and decorate with currants as desired.

◆ Cover with a towel and repeat with remaining dough. Let the breads rise in a warm place until almost doubled, about 30 minutes.

◆ Preheat oven to 350°F. Brush breads with the egg wash. Sprinkle with cinnamon sugar, if desired. Bake for 30 minutes, or until golden brown. Cool for 10 minutes on a rack.

◆ Serve warm or cool completely.

Crookneck squash frittata for two

MAKES 2 GENEROUS SERVINGS

2 teaspoons olive oil

2 tablespoons chopped onion or sliced green onions

¼ pound mushrooms, thinly sliced

1 medium crookneck squash or zucchini, thinly sliced

1 cup chopped tender chard leaves or spinach

1 tablespoon minced fresh parsley

½ teaspoon minced fresh basil or oregano

Salt and freshly ground black pepper

3 large eggs, lightly beaten with 2 teaspoons water

2 to 3 tablespoons shredded Gruyére or Parmesan cheese

Serve this frittata for breakfast, brunch, or a simple dinner. You might have most of these ingredients in your summer garden. Garnish with cherry tomatoes or with salsa.

◆ Heat the olive oil in a 10-inch nonstick skillet over medium-high heat. Add the onion and mushrooms and sauté for 2 minutes. Add the squash, chard, parsley, basil, and salt and pepper, to taste. Sauté for about 2 minutes, or until the vegetables are crisp-tender. Pour in the eggs, cover, and cook for about 2 minutes, or until eggs are almost set.

◆ If you have a broilerproof skillet, sprinkle the frittata with cheese and broil until set. If not, position a plate over the skillet and turn over. Slide the frittata, cooked side up, back into the skillet. Sprinkle with cheese, cover, and cook for 1 or 2 minutes more, or until the cheese melts.

◆ Cut into wedges and serve warm or at room temperature.

Spicy date mini loaves

A perfect host or hostess gift any time of year. If you prefer, you can make one large, nine-inch loaf; bake it for 60 to 65 minutes.

MAKES 3 SMALL LOAVES

1 cup all-purpose flour
⅔ cup whole wheat flour
1 teaspoon baking soda
1 teaspoon ground cinnamon
½ teaspoon ground cloves
¼ teaspoon ground allspice
¼ teaspoon salt
1¼ cups pumpkin or winter squash purée, canned or homemade (see Two-Way Winter Squash Purée, page 34)
½ cup (packed) brown sugar
1 egg, lightly beaten
¼ cup plain low-fat yogurt
2 tablespoons vegetable oil
½ cup chopped dates
1 tablespoon hulled pumpkin seeds or pine nuts

◆ Preheat oven to 350°F . Combine the all-purpose flour, whole wheat flour, baking soda, cinnamon, cloves, allspice, and salt in a medium bowl. Set aside.

◆ Combine the pumpkin purée, brown sugar, egg, yogurt, oil, and dates in a large bowl. Add the flour mixture and stir just until moistened.

◆ Spoon into 3 greased 5¾-by-3¼-by-2-inch loaf pans. Sprinkle with pumpkin seeds. Bake for 35 to 40 minutes, or until a wooden toothpick inserted near the center comes out clean. Cool in the pan for 5 minutes. Unmold onto a rack to cool thoroughly.

◆ Cut into thin slices to serve.

Pumpkin-orange pancakes with orange butter

MAKES ABOUT 24 THREE-INCH PANCAKES

1 large egg

½ cup buttermilk

½ cup pumpkin or winter squash purée, canned or homemade (see Two-Way Winter Squash Purée, page 34)

1 teaspoon grated orange peel

½ cup orange juice

1 tablespoon oil or melted butter

⅔ cup all-purpose flour

⅔ cup yellow cornmeal

2 tablespoons sugar

2 teaspoons baking powder

½ teaspoon salt

Vegetable oil for brushing griddle

Orange Butter (see method)

ORANGE BUTTER

Makes about ½ cup

4 tablespoons (½ stick) butter at room temperature

1 cup confectioners' sugar

2 teaspoons grated orange peel

If the pancake batter seems a little too thick, my husband, the pancake pro, suggests adding a little more orange juice. These golden pancakes are good with maple syrup too.

◆ Whisk together the egg, buttermilk, pumpkin purée, orange peel, orange juice, and oil in a large bowl. Combine the flour, cornmeal, sugar, baking powder, and salt in a medium bowl. Add to the pumpkin mixture and stir until blended.

◆ Heat a griddle over medium heat. Brush lightly with oil. Spoon a generous tablespoon of batter per pancake onto the griddle. Cook about 2 minutes on each side, or until browned and cooked through.

◆ Continue with remaining batter. Serve the pancakes warm with Orange Butter (see below).

◆ To make the Orange Butter: Combine the butter, confectioners' sugar, and orange peel in a small bowl. Beat until smooth. Serve at room temperature.

Note: The Orange Butter can be made ahead and refrigerated for up to 5 days. Bring to room temperature before serving.

Pumpkin sunflower seed waffles

MAKES ABOUT 8 SEVEN-INCH ROUND WAFFLES

1¾ cups all-purpose flour

⅓ cup white or yellow cornmeal

¼ cup (packed) light brown sugar

2 teaspoons baking powder

1½ teaspoons ground cinnamon

½ teaspoon ground ginger

½ teaspoon baking soda

¼ teaspoon salt

3 large eggs, separated

1¾ cups milk

1 cup pumpkin or winter squash purée, canned or homemade (see Two-Way Winter Squash Purée, page 34)

½ cup buttermilk or plain low-fat yogurt

⅓ cup canola oil

½ cup sunflower seeds

3 large bananas, sliced, or 2½ cups blueberries for topping (optional)

Maple syrup for serving

A lively crunch of sunflower seeds dots these lightly spiced waffles, ready to top with maple syrup or sliced bananas for a hearty breakfast or brunch. Make them up in advance, if you wish, freeze them, and reheat in a toaster oven at 300°F until hot through. To achieve a crispy texture, bake them on medium, rather than high, heat.

◆ Preheat a waffle iron. In a large bowl, whisk together the flour, cornmeal, sugar, baking powder, cinnamon, ginger, baking soda, and salt. In a medium bowl, beat the egg whites with an electric mixer until soft glossy peaks form. In another medium bowl, beat or whisk together the egg yolks, milk, pumpkin purée, buttermilk, and oil. Add the milk mixture to the dry ingredients and mix just until combined. Fold in the egg whites.

◆ Spoon or pour about 1 cup batter onto the hot iron. Sprinkle with 1 tablespoon sunflower seeds. Close the lid. Bake until the waffle is golden brown, 4 to 5 minutes. Remove with a fork to a warm plate. Serve at once or keep warm on a baking sheet in a 200°F oven.

◆ Repeat with the remaining batter. Top with sliced bananas or blueberries, if desired, and maple syrup.

Spaghetti squash hash browns

A great take on an American classic—glorious, golden comfort food. Try these easy hash browns for breakfast, dinner, or even a midnight snack.

MAKES 4 SERVINGS

4 to 5 cups (packed) cooked and shredded spaghetti squash (see Cooked Spaghetti Squash, page 22)

2 to 4 tablespoons finely chopped onion

2 to 3 tablespoons shredded Monterey Jack or Parmesan cheese (optional)

2 tablespoons all-purpose flour

¼ teaspoon salt

¼ teaspoon freshly ground black pepper

1 to 3 tablespoons butter, olive oil, or bacon drippings

1 teaspoon minced fresh chives or parsley (optional)

◆ Combine the spaghetti squash, onion, cheese (if using), flour, salt, and pepper in a large bowl. Heat the butter in a large skillet over medium heat. Add the squash mixture to the pan and pat into a cake. Cook, shaking the pan occasionally to prevent sticking, until the bottom is crisp and brown, about 10 minutes. Cut into quarters and turn over. Continue cooking until the bottom is crisp and brown, about 5 to 10 minutes longer.

◆ Serve on warm plates and sprinkle with chives, if desired.

Cooked spaghetti squash

MAKES 4 TO 5 CUPS

1 medium (about 3 pounds) spaghetti squash

Serve a pasta sauce over cooked spaghetti squash for an easy and healthful meal.

◆ Cut the squash in half lengthwise and scrape out the seeds. Pierce the skin several times with a kitchen fork.

◆ Oven directions: Preheat the oven to 350°F. Place the squash, cut side down, in a large baking dish. Bake for 50 to 70 minutes, or until the strands can be easily scraped from the shell with a table fork.

◆ Microwave directions: Place one half of the squash, cut side up, in a large microwave-safe dish or on a paper towel. Microwave at "high" (100%), rotating the dish once, for about 15 minutes, or until the strands can be easily scraped from the shell with a table fork. Repeat with the remaining half.

Note: Cooked spaghetti squash can be refrigerated, covered, for up to 2 days.

Pumpkin ginger smoothie

What fun it is to discover the hot sweet bite of ginger in this creamy morning beverage. Top it with granola for a healthy start to the day. Plan to freeze the banana in advance so it is ready for blending.

MAKES TWO 10-OUNCE DRINKS

- 1 large banana, peeled and frozen
- ⅔ cup plain yogurt
- ½ cup orange juice
- 2 teaspoons minced fresh ginger
- ½ cup pumpkin purée (see Two-Way Winter Squash Purée, page 34)
- Granola for topping

◆ Slice the frozen banana into ½-inch chunks. Put the banana, yogurt, orange juice, ginger, and pumpkin into a blender and blend until smooth. Pour into 2 glasses and serve with granola sprinkled over.

Two-way pumpkin yeast dough

MAKES 4 HALLOWEEN BREADS OR 2 COFFEE CAKE WREATHS

6¼ to 6¾ cups all-purpose flour

¾ cup (packed) light brown sugar

2 packages fast-rising yeast

1 teaspoon salt

1 teaspoon ground cinnamon

½ teaspoon ground nutmeg

1¼ cups milk

4 tablespoons (½ stick) butter

1 cup pumpkin or winter squash purée, canned or homemade (see Two-Way Winter Squash Purée, page 34)

3 large eggs, lightly beaten

1 teaspoon vanilla extract

Kids will have fun with this easy-to-work-with yeast dough. Shape into Halloween pumpkin breads or, with the help of an adult, almond-filled wreaths.

◆ Combine 3 cups of the flour, the brown sugar, yeast, salt, cinnamon, and nutmeg in the large bowl of an electric mixer. Heat the milk and butter in a saucepan or microwave to 120 to 130° F. Pour over the flour mixture and beat for 1 minute. Add the pumpkin purée, eggs, and vanilla and beat for 2 minutes more at medium speed. Gradually stir in enough of the remaining flour to make a soft dough. Knead with a dough hook or by hand on a floured surface until smooth and elastic. Place in an oiled bowl, cover, and let rise in a warm place until doubled, about 1 hour.

◆ Punch down the dough and knead briefly on a floured surface.

◆ To continue, see Almond-Pumpkin Coffee Cake Wreaths or Halloween Jack-o'-Lantern Breads (pages 10, 13).

Note: At this point, half or all of the dough can be placed in a plastic bag and refrigerated for up to 24 hours. Bring to room temperature before using.

SOUPS, STARTERS, AND PURÉES

Curried summer squash soup

MAKES 6 SERVINGS

- 4 tablespoons (½ stick) butter
- 1 medium onion, thinly sliced
- 1½ to 2 teaspoons garam masala (see Note)
- 2 teaspoons curry powder
- 2 cans (14½ ounces each) chicken broth or 4 cups homemade broth
- 4 cups sliced crookneck or other summer squash (about 1½ pounds)
- ½ cup plain yogurt or sour cream for serving
- ¼ cup toasted pistachios or almonds, chopped, for serving

Greg Atkinson, chef at Friday Harbor House on San Juan Island, Washington, suggests this robust soup with Indian flavors as a great use for those inevitable overgrown summer squash.

◆ Heat the butter in a skillet over medium heat. Add the onion and sauté for 10 minutes, or until golden brown. Stir in the garam masala and curry powder and cook for 1 minute more. Stir in the broth, add the squash, and bring the mixture to a boil. Reduce the heat to low and cook for 10 minutes, or until squash is tender. Transfer a third of the soup to a food processor or blender and purée until smooth. Repeat twice with the remaining soup. If necessary, reheat the soup.

◆ Serve hot with dollops of yogurt and a sprinkle of chopped pistachios.

Note: Garam masala, a blend of spices, varies considerably in strength. You can substitute a mixture of equal parts (half a teaspoon each) ground cardamom, coriander, cumin, and allspice.

Creamy winter squash soup with spices

MAKES 8 TO 10 SERVINGS

- 4 pounds assorted winter squashes, such as turban, Hubbard, or Australian Blue
- 1 tablespoon ground cumin
- 1 tablespoon ground coriander
- 2 teaspoons minced fresh sage or ¾ teaspoon dried rubbed sage
- 1½ teaspoons ground mace
- 3 tablespoons olive oil
- 1½ tablespoons minced fresh hot chile, such as jalapeño (see Note)
- 1 large onion, finely chopped
- 1 tart apple, such as Gravenstein or Granny Smith, cored, peeled, and grated
- 3 cans (14½ ounces each) chicken or vegetable broth
- Salt and freshly ground black pepper
- 1 cup cream, sour cream, or plain yogurt
- Croutons, fresh sage leaves, or whipped cream for garnish (optional)

Walter Bronowitz, Chef-Instructor at Edmonds Community College, makes a huge pot of this mixed squash soup every year at Seattle's Pike Place Market Labor Day Festival. He explains how to "temper" the soup to prevent it from curdling.

◆ Preheat oven to 375°F. Cut the squashes in half and scoop out the seeds and fibers. Place, cut side down, on a large, shallow baking pan. Bake for 45 to 75 minutes, or until very soft. Let cool, then scrape the squash meat from the skin. Discard the skin and mash the squash. Set aside.

◆ While the squash is baking, combine the cumin and coriander in a dry sauté pan. Toast, stirring constantly, until the spices change color and begin to smoke. Immediately remove from the pan and let cool in a small bowl. Add the sage and mace.

◆ Heat the olive oil over medium heat in a large heavy saucepan. Add the chiles and sauté for 5 minutes. Add the onion, partially cover, and continue to cook, stirring occasionally, until soft but not brown, about 5 minutes. Stir in the spice mixture. Add the apple. Increase the heat and cook, uncovered, stirring until the apple mixture becomes dry and begins to brown. Add the broth and scrape up the ingredients from the bottom of the pan with a wooden spoon. Stir in the mashed squash, bring to a simmer, and cook for 30 minutes. Purée the soup in a blender or food processor in several batches. Strain the soup, if desired. Season with salt and pepper to taste. (Refrigerate or freeze soup at this point, if desired.) Return soup to the pan. Reheat if necessary.

◆ Put the cream in a large bowl and gradually whisk in 1 cup of the hot soup. Then whisk in 2 more cups of the hot soup. Continue adding the hot soup until the outside of the bowl feels hot. Transfer the contents of the bowl back to the pan.

◆ Serve immediately or keep warm over low heat. Do not boil. Garnish with croutons, fresh sage, or whipped cream, if desired.

Note: Wear rubber gloves when chopping chiles.

Sautéed squash blossom appetizers

I am indebted to the mother of Chronicle Books editor Leslie Jonath for this sophisticated recipe. It calls for three herbs that thrive in most summer gardens.

MAKES 12 APPETIZERS

- 12 large squash blossoms
- 2 tablespoons finely chopped fresh basil
- 2 tablespoons finely chopped fresh flat-leaf parsley
- 1 tablespoon finely chopped fresh chives or green onion
- ½ teaspoon freshly ground black pepper
- 8 ounces fresh mozzarella, cut into 12 1-by-½-by-½-inch fingers
- 1 egg (or 2 eggs, if blossoms are very large), lightly beaten
- 2 teaspoons water
- ⅛ teaspoon salt, or to taste
- ½ cup all-purpose flour
- 2 to 3 tablespoons olive oil
- Lemon wedges for serving (optional)

◆ Remove and discard the stems from the squash blossoms. Set aside the blossoms. Combine the basil, parsley, chives, and pepper in a shallow dish. Coat each cheese finger with the herb mixture and place in a squash blossom. Twist to close. Combine the egg, water, and salt in a shallow dish. Put the flour in another shallow dish. Coat the blossoms with the egg mixture, then roll in the flour. Place on a tray. Blossoms can be refrigerated, covered, for up to 2 hours.

◆ Heat the oil in a large skillet over medium-high heat. Place as many blossoms into the skillet as fit easily. Cook, turning occasionally, for 3 to 5 minutes, or until golden brown. Drain on paper towels. Place in a low oven until all are cooked.

◆ Serve warm, with lemon wedges, if desired.

Corn chowder in miniature pumpkin shells

Whimsical little pumpkins filled with a cream soup make a perfect starter on Thanksgiving.

MAKES 4 SERVINGS

4 mini-pumpkins or Carnival, Sweet Dumpling, or acorn squashes ($\frac{3}{4}$ to 1$\frac{1}{4}$ pounds each)

1 slice bacon, diced

$\frac{1}{4}$ cup finely chopped onion

1 tablespoon all-purpose flour

$\frac{1}{2}$ teaspoon chili powder

1 cup chicken broth

Boiling water for heating pumpkin shells

1 cup corn kernels

$\frac{3}{4}$ cup milk

Flat-leaf parsley leaves for garnish (optional)

◆ With a small sharp knife, cut wide tops out of the pumpkins to make bowl-shaped shells. Scrape out and discard seeds and fibers. Trim all but $\frac{1}{4}$ inch of meat from tops. Using a knife and soup spoon, cut and scrape out some of the pumpkin meat, leaving a $\frac{3}{8}$-inch-thick shell. (Shells should have about a $\frac{3}{4}$-cup capacity.) Chop the pumpkin meat and set aside.

◆ Stove-top directions: Sauté the bacon in a saucepan for 3 minutes, or until crisp. Remove the bacon and set aside. Add the onion and chopped pumpkin meat to the saucepan. Sauté over medium heat until tender, about 10 minutes. Stir in the flour and chili powder, then the chicken broth. Cook for 5 minutes more, or until the pumpkin is very soft. Meanwhile, pour boiling water into the pumpkin shells to warm them. Mash the pumpkin mixture with a fork to a coarse purée. Add the corn and milk. Continue to cook until thoroughly heated.

◆ Microwave directions: Put the bacon in a 2-quart microwave-safe dish. Microwave at "high" (100%) for 1 minute and 45 seconds to 2 minutes, or until crisp, stirring twice. Remove the bacon and set aside. Add the onion and chopped pumpkin meat to the dish. Cover with the lid or vented heavy-duty plastic wrap and microwave at "high" for 2 minutes, or until soft. Stir in the flour and chili powder, then the chicken broth. Microwave, covered, at "high" for 5 minutes, or until the pumpkin is very soft. Meanwhile, pour boiling water into the pumpkin shells to warm them. Mash the pumpkin mixture with a fork to a coarse purée. Add the corn and milk. Microwave at "high" for 1 to 2 minutes, or until thoroughly heated.

◆ Empty and dry the pumpkin shells. Fill with the chowder. Sprinkle the bacon on top and garnish with parsley, if desired. Serve at once.

Two-way winter squash purée

MAKES ABOUT 2 CUPS PURÉE

About 2 pounds butternut or acorn squash or small sugar pumpkin

It is easier to bake a large squash or pumpkin in a conventional oven. A small two-pound pumpkin, however, cooks faster in a microwave oven. Homemade purées tend to be bright yellow-orange, rather than the orange color of most canned pumpkin. Each squash has its own unique flavor.

◆ Cut the squash in half and scrape out the seeds and fibers.

◆ Oven directions: Preheat oven to 350°F. Place the squash, cut side down, on a large, shallow baking pan. Bake, uncovered, for 50 to 70 minutes, or until the squash is fork tender. Let cool.

◆ Microwave directions: Cut the squash halves into one-inch slices or ¼-pound chunks. Peel if desired. Place, cut side down, in a microwave-safe dish. Cover with a lid or vented heavy-duty plastic wrap. Microwave at "high" (100%) for 15 minutes, or until the meat is fork tender, rearranging the squash once. In general, allow 7 to 10 minutes microwaving time per pound. Let cool.

◆ To make the purée: Drain off any liquid and scoop the pulp from the skins. Purée the pulp in a food processor or blender, pulsing on and off until smooth. (Or mash thoroughly with a potato masher or pass through a food mill.) Scoop the purée into a strainer and allow it to drain for at least 30 minutes, or until it is as thick as canned purée or mashed potatoes. (Purée can be refrigerated, covered, for up to 2 days or frozen, well wrapped, for several months. The most convenient size of container is ½ cup.)

Note: A 4½ pound pumpkin or winter squash yields about 4 cups of purée. Although nothing tops the flavor of homemade pumpkin or winter squash purée, you can substitute canned purée when using it as an ingredient in other recipes.

Winter squash ravioli

One Christmas we were lucky enough to stay and eat at Da Bebbe Sello in Cortina d'Ampezzo, Italy. These raviolis are a simplified version of what we were served. Wonton wrappers are a real labor- and time-saver, as is a two-part pasta cooker with a drainer that lifts out of the pot.

MAKES 24 RAVIOLI, 4 TO 6 SERVINGS

- ¼ cup hazelnuts
- ½ cup butternut, kabocha, banana, or other winter squash purée, canned or homemade (see Two-Way Winter Squash Purée, page 34)
- ½ cup low-fat ricotta cheese
- ¼ teaspoon freshly ground black pepper
- ⅛ teaspoon salt
- Dash of nutmeg, preferably fresh grated
- ¼ to ½ teaspoon finely minced fresh sage (optional)
- 24 (3-by-3-inch) wonton skins, thawed if necessary
- Wax paper
- Cornmeal for dusting
- 3 tablespoons butter
- Minced fresh parsley for garnish
- Freshly grated Parmesan cheese for serving

◆ Preheat oven to 350°F. On a baking sheet, toast the hazelnuts for 10 minutes, shaking occasionally. Let cool. Finely chop and set aside.

◆ Combine the squash purée, ricotta, pepper, salt, nutmeg, and sage (if using) in a medium bowl. Drop a rounded teaspoon of the squash mixture onto each of 4 wonton skins. With your finger, lightly moisten 2 edges of each wonton skin with water. Fold into a triangle and press to seal. Continue with the remaining wonton skins and filling. Layer between sheets of wax paper sprinkled with cornmeal.

◆ Bring a large pot of salted water to a boil. Cook the ravioli, twelve at a time, for about 3 minutes, or until the ravioli begin to look transparent. Carefully lift from the water and drain.

◆ As the ravioli cook, heat 1 tablespoon of the butter in a skillet. Add the first batch of drained ravioli and sauté for 2 to 3 minutes. Arrange the ravioli on a warmed platter or on plates. Cover and keep warm.

◆ Repeat with the remaining ravioli.

◆ Heat the remaining 2 tablespoons of butter in the skillet. Add the hazelnuts and heat briefly.

◆ Sprinkle the nuts and then the parsley over the ravioli. Serve with Parmesan cheese.

Pumpkin with browned butter, sage, and asiago

An excellent fillip to sugar pumpkin or butternut squash is a finish of browned butter, crispy fresh sage, and shavings of Asiago cheese. It makes an ideal side dish to roast turkey, duck, or pork loin.

MAKES 4 SERVINGS

1 medium (about 2 pounds) sugar pumpkin or butternut squash

4 tablespoons (½ stick) unsalted butter

8 to 10 fresh sage leaves, minced

¼ teaspoon freshly grated nutmeg

Sea salt and freshly ground black pepper

1½ ounces Asiago, Parmesan, or Grana cheese, cut into shavings (about ⅓ cup)

◆ Preheat the oven to 400°F. Split the pumpkin in half lengthwise and scoop out and discard the seeds and fibers. Place cut side down on a greased baking sheet with a rim and bake until fork tender, 40 to 50 minutes. Remove from the oven, let cool slightly, and cut into serving-size pieces. Scoop the pumpkin from the shell and place on a serving dish.

◆ In a small saucepan, melt the butter over medium heat and heat until it starts to brown. Pour about 3 tablespoons over the pumpkin. Add the sage to the remaining butter in the pan and heat until the sage crisps. Spoon over the pumpkin and season with nutmeg and salt and pepper, to taste. Scatter the cheese over.

Spaghetti squash with mushroom sauce

MAKES 4 APPETIZER OR 2 ENTRÉE SERVINGS

½ medium (3- to 4-pound) spaghetti squash, cut lengthwise

2 tablespoons butter

1 tablespoon olive oil

¼ cup finely chopped shallots

2 large portobello mushrooms, stems removed and reserved for another use, cut into ½-inch-thick slices and each slice halved

4 large cremini or white button mushrooms, cut into ¼-inch-thick slices

⅓ cup dry white wine

2 tablespoons minced fresh flat-leaf parsley

⅛ teaspoon fresh thyme

¼ cup heavy cream

Salt and freshly ground black pepper

Should you miss the chanterelle or porcini season, you'll find commercially grown portobellos and cremini available year-round. Serve with a crusty bread. The recipe can be doubled by using two skillets or a very large one.

◆ Cook the spaghetti squash (see Cooked Spaghetti Squash, page 22).

◆ Heat the butter and oil in a large skillet over medium heat. Add the shallots and sauté for about 5 minutes, or until golden. Add the mushrooms and sauté about 5 minutes more, or until soft. Stir in the wine and cook until the liquid is reduced to about 3 tablespoons. Stir in the parsley and thyme. Add the cream and heat until warmed through. Season with salt and pepper, to taste.

◆ Spoon the mushroom sauce over the hot spaghetti squash. Serve warm.

Lentil and pumpkin sun-dried tomato salad

MAKES 8 TO 10 SERVINGS

1 pound small green or brown lentils

1 medium yellow onion, chopped

1 carrot, shredded (optional)

5 cups water

2 cloves garlic, minced

½ teaspoon dried thyme

1 bay leaf

Salt and freshly ground black pepper

1½ pounds (1½ cups) peeled, diced pumpkin or butternut squash

3 tablespoons olive oil

¼ cup balsamic vinegar

8 sun-dried oil-cured tomatoes, snipped into pieces

2 ounces (½ cup) diced feta cheese

½ cup minced green onion tops, chives, flat-leaf parsley, and basil or oregano

This hearty salad is great for a potluck or picnic. Or let it serve as a vegetarian entrée. It is important not to overcook the lentils. They should still have some tooth. Another option instead of using the sun-dried tomatoes is to substitute half a cup of dried cranberries.

◆ Into a saucepot, add the lentils, onion, carrot, water, garlic, thyme, bay leaf, and salt and pepper, to taste. Cover and simmer for 20 to 25 minutes, or until lentils are just slightly crunchy. Remove bay leaf.

◆ Meanwhile, put the pumpkin in a microwavable dish, cover with plastic wrap, and microwave 10 minutes, or until just cooked through. Or steam the pumpkin over simmering water for 15 minutes, or until tender. Toss with 1 tablespoon of the olive oil. Drain the lentils and put into a large bowl. Add a mixture of vinegar, the remaining 2 tablespoons oil, and salt and pepper to taste. Stir in the pumpkin and tomatoes. Sprinkle with feta and herbs. Chill 1 hour or up to 1 day before serving.

ENTRÉES AND SIDE DISHES

Vegetarian summer squash lasagne

MAKES 8 SERVINGS

2 large (about 1½ pounds) yellow straightneck squash, trimmed and thinly sliced

1 tablespoon salt

TOMATO-MUSHROOM SAUCE

1 tablespoon olive oil

1 medium onion, chopped

1 red bell pepper, cored, seeded, and thinly sliced

½ pound mushrooms, sliced

1 tablespoon flour

1 can (28 ounces) crushed tomatoes in tomato purée

1 tablespoon minced fresh basil

2 teaspoons minced fresh oregano

Salt and freshly ground black pepper

CHEESE FILLING

About 2 cups (15-ounce carton) low-fat ricotta cheese

1 package (10 ounces) frozen chopped spinach, thawed and squeezed dry

2 tablespoons chopped fresh flat-leaf parsley

4 ounces part-skim-milk mozzarella, thinly sliced

Lasagne is a year-round dish. This version started out one Christmas Eve with a special request from a vegetarian niece. It's fresh tasting and very low in fat. If straightneck squash is unavailable, crookneck can be used.

◆ Spread the sliced squash in a large shallow dish. Sprinkle evenly with salt and let stand for about 25 minutes, turning occasionally. Rinse thoroughly in a colander and pat dry with a towel. Set aside.

◆ To make the sauce: Heat the olive oil in a large skillet over medium heat. Add the onion and bell pepper and sauté until the onion is golden, about 7 minutes. Stir in the mushrooms and continue to cook for 5 minutes more. Add the flour and mix well. Stir in the tomatoes, basil, and oregano. Season with salt and pepper, to taste. Bring to a boil, reduce the heat, and simmer uncovered for 20 minutes, or until slightly thickened. Set aside. (Makes about 5 cups of sauce.)

◆ To make the filling: Combine the ricotta, spinach, and parsley. Set aside.

◆ Preheat oven to 375°F. Spread a fourth of the tomato-mushroom sauce in a 13-by-9-by-2-inch baking dish. Arrange a third of the squash evenly over the sauce. Dollop with half of the cheese mixture. Add another fourth of the tomato sauce, another third of the squash, and the remaining cheese mixture. Cover with another fourth of the tomato sauce, the remaining squash, and then the remaining tomato sauce. Bake for 20 minutes.

◆ Arrange the mozzarella slices on top. Continue to bake for 25 minutes more, or until the lasagne bubbles and is hot in the center.

◆ Let stand for 15 minutes before serving.

Pomegranate chicken with pumpkin and sage

This is an excellent dish for guests, as the chicken may be assembled in advance and the pumpkin steamed ahead of time. Pomegranate juice, readily available in markets, adds a piquant flavor to the dish.

MAKES 4 SERVINGS

- 2 teaspoons olive oil
- 1 large yellow onion, finely chopped
- 3 cloves garlic, minced
- ⅓ cup dry red wine
- 2 tablespoons balsamic vinegar
- ½ cup pomegranate juice
- 1 teaspoon Dijon mustard
- 1 teaspoon maple syrup
- 8 large chicken thighs (about 2½ pounds)
- Salt and freshly ground black pepper
- 1 medium (about 2 pounds) sugar pumpkin or butternut squash
- 2 tablespoons unsalted butter
- 6 sage leaves, minced

◆ Preheat the oven to 375°F. In a small saucepan, heat the oil over medium heat and sauté the onion and garlic until soft, about 10 minutes. Add the wine and vinegar and reduce slightly. Add the juice, mustard, and maple syrup and simmer to blend.

◆ Arrange the chicken in a baking dish, spoon the sauce over, and season with salt and pepper. Bake in the oven for 30 to 35 minutes, or until cooked through.

◆ Meanwhile, peel the pumpkin, halve, and remove the seeds and fibers. Slice into ½-inch crescents. Steam over simmering water for 15 to 20 minutes, or until tender when pierced with a fork. Transfer to a serving dish. In a small saucepan, heat the butter and sage until the sage crisps. Spoon over the pumpkin and season with salt and pepper, to taste.

◆ On each serving plate arrange two chicken thighs with a crescent of pumpkin slices surrounding them.

Roasted herb chicken with autumn vegetables

MAKES 4 OR 5 SERVINGS

1 whole frying chicken (3½ to 4 pounds)

8 to 10 fresh sage leaves or ¼ teaspoon dried sage

2 tablespoons olive oil

1 tablespoon red wine vinegar

1 teaspoon Dijon mustard

1½ teaspoons minced fresh thyme or ½ teaspoon dried thyme

1½ teaspoons minced fresh oregano or ½ teaspoon dried oregano

1½ pounds Hubbard, banana, turban, buttercup, calabaza, and/or other winter squash, seeded, rind removed, and meat cut into 2-by-½-inch strips

12 to 15 small new potatoes, scrubbed, or about 1¼ pounds large potatoes, scrubbed and cut into 1-inch chunks

1 large onion, cut into wedges

Sprigs of fresh sage, thyme, and/or oregano for garnish (optional)

Whenever I get a chance to go home, I ask for Mom's roast chicken. It doesn't take her long to put the dish together, using the vegetables on hand. Then she's back to her true vocation, gardening.

◆ Preheat oven to 375°F. Remove the chicken neck and giblets. Loosen the skin from the breast with your fingers and insert the sage leaves under the skin or sprinkle dried sage under the skin.

◆ Combine the oil, vinegar, mustard, thyme, and oregano in a large bowl. Rub some of the mixture onto the chicken. Place chicken, breast side down, in a large, shallow roasting pan. Toss the vegetables with the remaining herb mixture and arrange in the roasting pan.

◆ Roast for 30 minutes. Turn the chicken over and stir the vegetables. Continue to cook for about 45 minutes more, or until an instant-read thermometer inserted in the thickest part of the thigh reads 185°F, the meat near the thigh bone is no longer pink, and the vegetables are tender.

◆ Transfer the chicken to a large platter and surround with the vegetables. Garnish with herbs, if desired. Carve and serve.

Butternut risotto

MAKES 4 TO 6 SERVINGS

1 can (14½ ounces) chicken broth or 2 cups homemade broth

3 cups water

2 to 3 tablespoons olive oil

¼ cup finely chopped onion

3 cups shredded butternut or other winter squash

1 cup Arborio rice

½ cup dry white wine

2 tablespoons freshly grated Parmesan cheese, plus more for sprinkling

Salt and freshly ground black pepper

To me, risotto is food for the soul. I prefer butternut squash for its subtle, nutty flavor, but other winter squash can be used.

◆ Heat the chicken broth and water in a saucepan to a slow simmer.

◆ Heat the olive oil in a heavy saucepan over medium-high heat. Add the onion and cook until translucent, about 5 minutes. Add the shredded squash and cook over medium heat, stirring frequently with a wooden spatula or spoon, until lightly browned, 10 to 15 minutes. Add the rice and cook for 1 minute, stirring constantly. Add the wine and cook and stir until the liquid has evaporated. Add ½ cup of the broth mixture and cook, stirring constantly, until the liquid is absorbed. Continue stirring in the broth, ½ cup at a time, until all or most of the liquid has been absorbed and the rice is tender but still al dente, 20 to 25 minutes. Stir in the Parmesan. Season with salt and pepper, to taste.

◆ Sprinkle Parmesan on top and serve.

Note: Serve the risotto as a first course, as in Italy, or as a side dish.

Pattypan pita bread pizzas

Looking for a quick lunch, a late supper, or a fancy hors d'oeuvre? These colorful mini-pizzas will fit the bill.

MAKES 4 SMALL PIZZAS

- **2 pita breads (6-inch size), each separated into 2 rounds**
- **3 tablespoons olive oil**
- **1 large red bell pepper, cored, seeded, and thinly sliced**
- **1 small onion, thinly sliced**
- **1 pound pattypan or other summer squash, trimmed and cut into ½-inch slices**
- **1 tablespoon minced fresh basil or 1 teaspoon dried basil**
- **¼ teaspoon salt**
- **¼ teaspoon freshly ground black pepper**
- **½ cup ricotta cheese**
- **6 black olives, pitted and sliced**
- **Crushed red pepper**

◆ Preheat oven to 350°F. Brush the rough side of the pitas lightly with a little olive oil. Place oiled side up on a baking sheet and bake for 5 minutes. Set aside to cool.

◆ Heat the remaining oil in a large skillet over medium heat. Add the bell pepper and onion and sauté for 4 minutes. Add the squash, basil, salt, and pepper. Cook for 2 minutes more, or until vegetables are tender.

◆ Preheat the broiler. Arrange the vegetables on the pitas. Dollop with ricotta and sprinkle with black olives and crushed red pepper, to taste. Broil 4 to 6 inches from the heat for about 1 minute, or until the cheese has softened, the vegetables are heated through, and the bread is crisp.

◆ Cut into wedges to serve.

Chayote boats or zucchini slippers

The zucchini slipper idea came from Pidge Barry of Los Altos, California. I've adapted her zucchini recipe to suit the chayote. The whole vegetable is edible when cooked, including the seed.

MAKES 8 PIECES

4 chayotes (about 3 pounds) or 4 zucchini (about 2 pounds)

3/4 cup (about 3 ounces) shredded sharp Cheddar cheese

1/4 cup small-curd cottage cheese

1 egg, well beaten

1 tablespoon finely chopped fresh flat-leaf parsley

1 teaspoon minced fresh chives or green onion

1/2 teaspoon dried Italian seasoning

Salt and freshly ground black pepper

Paprika for garnish

◆ Place chayotes in boiling salted water. Cover, reduce the heat, and simmer for 25 to 35 minutes, or until tender when pierced with the point of a knife. If using zucchini, cook in simmering water for 4 to 5 minutes, or until tender. Drain the squash and let cool.

◆ Cut the squash in half lengthwise. For the chayote, remove and discard the seeds and seed casings. Cut with a grapefruit knife around the edge, leaving a 1/4-inch shell. Be careful not to cut through the skin. Lift out the pulp and finely chop it. Squeeze dry. If using zucchini, trim the ends and scoop out the seedy pulp in the center. Finely chop the pulp and squeeze dry.

◆ Preheat oven to 350°F. Oil a large baking sheet.

◆ For either type of squash, combine the squash pulp, Cheddar cheese, cottage cheese, egg, parsley, chives, and Italian seasoning in a medium bowl. Season with salt and pepper, to taste. Divide the filling among the squash halves, mounding as necessary. Place on the baking sheet and sprinkle with paprika. Bake, uncovered, for 10 to 15 minutes, or until heated through. Then broil 4 to 5 inches from the heat for 2 to 3 minutes, or until golden brown.

◆ Serve warm.

Moroccan beef and pumpkin tajine

MAKES 4 SERVINGS

2 tablespoons olive oil
1 large yellow onion, chopped
2 teaspoons minced fresh ginger
1 stick cinnamon
½ teaspoon ground allspice
½ teaspoon ground coriander
2 cloves garlic, minced
1½ pounds beef stew meat, cut into 1-inch cubes
⅓ cup dried cranberries
2 tablespoons dried sherry
1 medium (about 2 pounds) sugar pumpkin, peeled and cut into 1-inch cubes
1 tablespoon honey
1½ tablespoons fresh lime juice
2 tablespoons chopped pistachios
¼ cup chopped fresh cilantro
Lime wedges for garnish

A conical utensil called a tajine is used for cooking Moroccan meat and fruit stews. The delightful addition of pumpkin with spices, honey, citrus, and nuts provides a beautiful union of flavors.

◆ Preheat the oven to 325°F. In a heavy saucepot, heat the oil over medium heat and sauté the onion, ginger, cinnamon stick, allspice, and coriander until the onion is soft, about 10 minutes. Add the garlic and meat and sauté until the meat is browned, about 7 minutes, turning to coat all sides.

◆ Place the cranberries in a small dish and cover with sherry. Set aside.

◆ Cover and bake the meat in the oven for 30 minutes. Add the pumpkin and cranberries, cover, and bake 1 hour longer, or until the meat is tender. Add the honey and lime juice to the pan drippings and heat over medium high, scraping the bottom of the pan. Sprinkle with nuts and cilantro and garnish with lime wedges.

Grilled green and gold zucchini, santa fe style

Katharine Kagel serves this dish at Cafe Pasqual's in Santa Fe. Make a salad from the leftovers by chopping the vegetables and tossing them with a spoonful of balsamic vinegar, a handful of black olives, and a sprinkle of toasted sesame seeds.

MAKES 4 TO 6 SERVINGS

¼ cup olive oil

2 tablespoons balsamic vinegar

½ teaspoon minced garlic

½ teaspoon salt

½ teaspoon freshly ground black pepper

¼ teaspoon red pepper flakes

1 pound green zucchini, cut lengthwise into ¼- to ½-inch strips

1 large red bell pepper, cored, seeded, and cut lengthwise into ½-inch strips

◆ Combine the oil, vinegar, garlic, salt, pepper, and red pepper flakes in a large shallow dish. Add the vegetables and turn to coat. Marinate for 1 to 4 hours, turning occasionally.

◆ Prepare the grill (see Note).

◆ Grill over medium-hot coals, 4 to 6 inches from the heat, basting and turning once, until the squash is tender and streaked with brown, about 10 minutes total.

Note: The vegetables can also be cooked under a broiler.

Easy tortellini-zucchini combo

MAKES 2 SERVINGS

4 ounces (½ package) dried cheese-filled tortellini

1 to 2 teaspoons olive oil

1 small onion, halved and thinly sliced

2 medium or 1 large (½ pound) zucchini, halved lengthwise if large and cut into ¼-inch-thick slices

4 to 6 mushrooms, sliced

½ teaspoon dried basil, crushed

Salt and freshly ground black pepper

Shredded Parmesan cheese for serving

A super simple dinner that can be put together just about anywhere. It's great for camping, as nothing really requires refrigeration.

◆ Bring a large saucepan of salted water to a boil. Add the tortellini and boil for 15 to 25 minutes, or until tender (see Note).

◆ Meanwhile, heat the olive oil in a skillet over medium-high heat. Add the onion and sauté for about 2 minutes. Add the zucchini and sauté for 3 to 5 minutes, or until lightly browned. Add the mushrooms and continue to cook for 3 to 5 minutes, or until vegetables are tender. Season with basil and salt and pepper, to taste. Reduce the heat to low until the pasta is done.

◆ Drain the pasta, but not too thoroughly, and add the pasta to the skillet. Heat through. Serve with Parmesan cheese.

Note: It takes a lot longer at high altitudes for the pasta to cook.

DESSERTS

Old-fashioned sugar-pumpkin spice cake

MAKES ABOUT 12 SERVINGS

2 cups all-purpose flour

2 teaspoons baking powder

½ teaspoon baking soda

½ teaspoon salt

1¼ teaspoons ground cinnamon

½ teaspoon ground ginger

¼ teaspoon ground allspice

¼ teaspoon ground cloves

¼ teaspoon ground nutmeg

8 tablespoons (1 stick) butter at room temperature

1¼ cups sugar

1 large egg and 2 egg whites or 2 whole large eggs

1 teaspoon vanilla extract

1 cup pumpkin or winter squash purée, canned or homemade (see Two-Way Winter Squash Purée, page 34)

¾ cup low-fat milk

⅓ cup raisins or chocolate chips (optional)

Orange icing (see method)

1 ounce semisweet chocolate, chopped, for spider and web (optional)

This easy-to-make sheet cake with an orange-flavored frosting will be a year-round favorite. On Halloween you might want to add a chocolate spider in a chocolate spider web.

◆ Preheat oven to 350°F. Combine the flour, baking powder, baking soda, salt, cinnamon, ginger, allspice, cloves, and nutmeg in a large bowl. Set aside. Cream the butter in the large bowl of an electric mixer. Gradually beat in the sugar. Add the eggs, one at a time, and the vanilla. In a medium bowl, combine the purée and milk. Add the flour mixture alternately with the pumpkin mixture to the butter mixture, starting and ending with the flour mixture, and stirring just until blended.

◆ Stir in the raisins, if using. Spread the batter in a greased 13-by-9-by-2-inch pan. Bake for 30 minutes, or until a wooden toothpick inserted near the center comes out clean. Cool in the pan on a rack.

◆ Spread with orange icing (see below), while still in the pan. If desired, place the chocolate in a small sealable plastic bag. Immerse in warm water until melted. Snip off a tiny corner and pipe a chocolate spider and web onto the cake.

◆ To make the icing: In a medium bowl, beat together 4 tablespoons (½ stick) butter at room temperature, 1 teaspoon grated orange peel, and 2 cups sifted confectioners' sugar. Add enough orange juice to make a spreading consistency, 1½ to 2 tablespoons. Makes about 1 cup.

◆ Cut into squares to serve.

Pumpkin soufflé custard

MAKES 6 TO 8 SERVINGS

3 large eggs, separated

1/8 teaspoon cream of tartar

1/2 cup (packed) light brown sugar

1 1/2 teaspoons ground cinnamon

1 teaspoon ground ginger

1/4 teaspoon ground cloves

1/4 teaspoon salt

1 cup pumpkin or winter squash purée, canned or homemade (see Two-Way Winter Squash Purée, page 34)

1 cup milk

2 tablespoons butter, melted

Whipped cream flavored with chopped crystallized ginger or rum to serve (see method)

As it bakes, this pudding becomes a custard base topped with a spicy soufflé. It is ideal for the Thanksgiving dinner as a switch from the usual pumpkin pie. It is actually an old-fashioned favorite from decades ago.

◆ Preheat the oven to 375°F. Lightly butter a 1 1/2-quart baking dish or soufflé dish. In a medium bowl, beat the egg whites until foamy. Add the cream of tartar and beat until soft peaks form. Gradually beat in 1/4 cup of the brown sugar. Beat until it holds stiff upright peaks; set aside. In a large bowl, beat the egg yolks until light. Beat in the remaining 1/4 cup brown sugar, cinnamon, ginger, cloves, and salt. Stir in the pumpkin and milk. Fold one third of the egg white mixture into the egg yolk mixture. Blend until smooth. Gently fold in the remaining egg white mixture and the melted butter. Pour into the baking dish. Place the baking dish in a large baking pan. Pour in water to a depth of 1 inch. Bake for 35 to 40 minutes, or until a knife inserted in the center comes out clean. Cool slightly. Serve with flavored whipped cream (see below).

◆ To make the flavored whipped cream: In a small, deep bowl, whip 1 cup of heavy cream until stiff. Fold in 2 tablespoons of powdered sugar and 3 tablespoons of finely crystallized ginger or 2 tablespoons of dark rum.

Pumpkin eggnog bombe with caramelized pecans

A spicy pumpkin center fills this festive ice cream bombe. This is ideal for a busy holiday dinner, as it can be frozen several days in advance.

MAKES 8 TO 10 SERVINGS

1 quart vanilla or eggnog ice cream

2 cups pumpkin or winter squash purée, canned or homemade (see Two-Way Winter Squash Purée, page 34)

⅔ cup (packed) light brown sugar

1 teaspoon ground cinnamon

¼ teaspoon ground ginger

¼ teaspoon ground cloves

¼ teaspoon freshly grated nutmeg

¼ teaspoon salt

1 cup whipping cream

3 tablespoons Grand Marnier or rum

1 tablespoon unsalted butter

1 tablespoon sugar

½ cup chopped pecans

◆ Onto the bottom and sides of a 1½-quart ice cream mold or fluted salad mold, pack a ¾-inch-thick layer of ice cream. Put the mold into the freezer. Freeze until the ice cream is firm. In a large bowl, combine the pumpkin, sugar, cinnamon, ginger, cloves, nutmeg, and salt. In a medium bowl, whip the cream until soft peaks form and beat in the Grand Marnier. Fold the whipped cream mixture into the pumpkin mixture. Spoon the mixture into the center of the ice-cream-lined mold. Cover and freeze until firm, at least 8 hours.

◆ In a small saucepan, melt the butter over medium heat, add the sugar and pecans and heat, stirring, until the nuts are lightly toasted and caramelized.

◆ To unmold the bombe, dip the mold into a pan of hot water for 5 seconds. Invert on a serving platter. Cut into wedges and sprinkle with the caramelized nuts. Serve immediately.

Brazilian butternut flan

Clara, who lived next door to us in Rio de Janeiro, would buy a piece of squash at the outdoor market for her *pudim de abobora*, or pumpkin pudding. The supermarket also stocked canned pumpkin, with coconut or plain.

MAKES ABOUT 6 SERVINGS

1½ cups sugar

3 large eggs, beaten

1¼ cups milk, half-and-half, or canned evaporated milk

1¼ teaspoons vanilla extract

Dash of salt

1 cup butternut, calabaza, or other winter squash purée, canned or homemade (see Two-Way Winter Squash Purée, page 34)

◆ Place 1 cup of the sugar in a large heavy skillet over medium-high heat. Cook, without stirring, until the sugar begins to melt. Reduce the heat to low and cook and stir until it turns a golden brown, about 8 to 10 minutes. Quickly pour the caramel into a 9- or 10-inch (1-quart) deep-dish pie plate and tip to coat the bottom and sides.

◆ Preheat oven to 350°F. Put water on to boil.

◆ Beat the eggs with the remaining ½ cup sugar. Stir in the milk, vanilla, salt, and the squash purée. Strain the mixture and pour into the caramel-lined pan. Place in a large baking pan and add boiling water halfway up the side of the pie plate. Bake for 45 to 50 minutes, or until set in the center when gently shaken. Remove from the hot water and chill for at least 4 hours or overnight.

◆ To serve, loosen the custard with the tip of a knife. Place a platter on top and quickly turn over. Hold in place until the caramel flows out.

Pumpkin ice cream sundaes with pecan brittle

MAKES ABOUT 1¼ QUARTS

ICE CREAM

Yolks of 2 large eggs

¾ cup sugar

2 cups milk

1 cup pumpkin or winter squash purée, canned or homemade (see Two-Way Winter Squash Purée, page 34)

1½ teaspoons ground cinnamon

¼ teaspoon ground cloves

½ teaspoon ground ginger

½ teaspoon ground nutmeg

Dash of salt

1 cup heavy cream

¾ teaspoon vanilla extract

Softly whipped cream (optional)

Pecan Brittle (see method)

PECAN BRITTLE

Makes about 2 cups

½ cup pecans

Butter for greasing foil

1 cup sugar

Pumpkin ice cream is like a summertime pumpkin pie.

◆ To make the ice cream: Whisk together the egg yolks and sugar in a large bowl. Heat the milk in a large saucepan over medium-high heat until bubbles form around the edge. Slowly pour into the egg mixture, stirring constantly. Return the mixture to the saucepan. Reduce the heat to medium-low and cook, stirring, just until the mixture thickens and coats the back of a spoon. Do not overheat or custard may curdle.

◆ In a small bowl, combine the pumpkin purée and the cinnamon, cloves, ginger, nutmeg, and salt. Stir into the custard. Strain into a bowl. Stir in the cream and vanilla. Chill thoroughly. Freeze in an ice-cream maker according to manufacturer's directions.

◆ To make the Pecan Brittle: Heat oven to 325°F. Spread the pecans in a shallow pan and toast for 10 minutes, shaking the pan occasionally. Cool slightly and coarsely chop. Butter a large piece of foil. Heat the sugar in a large skillet over medium-high heat. Cook, shaking occasionally, until the sugar melts and turns amber. Stir in the pecans and pour out onto the prepared foil. Cool. Break brittle into pieces, reserving a few large pieces to top the sundaes. Place the remaining brittle in a heavy-duty plastic bag and crush with a rolling pin.

◆ Serve with softly whipped cream, if desired, and a sprinkle of Pecan Brittle.

Classic pumpkin-pecan pie

MAKES ONE 9- OR 10-INCH PIE

FLAKY PASTRY

1 cup all-purpose flour

¼ teaspoon salt

⅓ cup (5⅓ tablespoons) shortening or butter

3 to 3½ tablespoons ice water

PUMPKIN-PECAN FILLING

3 large eggs

1 cup pumpkin or winter squash purée, canned or homemade (see Two-Way Winter Squash Purée, page 34)

½ cup granulated sugar

⅔ cup evaporated regular or low-fat milk

¼ teaspoon freshly grated nutmeg

⅓ cup maple syrup

¼ cup (packed) dark brown sugar

1 tablespoon butter, melted

½ teaspoon vanilla extract

Dash of salt

¾ cup pecan halves

The best of all worlds: pumpkin pie and pecan pie layered in the same dish.

◆ To make the pastry: Combine the flour and salt in a small bowl. Cut in the shortening until mixture is the size of small peas. Gradually sprinkle in the water, 1 tablespoon at a time, until the mixture holds together when gathered with a fork. Press together into a disk, wrap in plastic wrap, and refrigerate for at least 20 minutes.

◆ To make the filling: Lightly beat 2 of the eggs in a medium bowl. Stir in the pumpkin purée, granulated sugar, evaporated milk, and nutmeg. Set aside. In another medium bowl, beat the remaining egg. Stir in the maple syrup, brown sugar, butter, vanilla, and salt. Mix well. Stir in the pecans.

◆ Preheat oven to 425°F. Roll out the pastry on a lightly floured surface to an 11- to 12-inch circle. Transfer to a 9- or 10-inch pie pan. Trim the crust allowing a ½-inch overhang. Fold under the edge and flute. Place on a baking sheet and pour in the pumpkin mixture. Bake for 25 minutes.

◆ Pour the pecan mixture over the pumpkin layer and spread evenly. Reduce the heat to 350°F and continue to bake for 20 minutes more, or until the filling is slightly puffed and a knife inserted near the center comes out clean. Cool on a rack.

◆ Serve within 4 hours or refrigerate, loosely covered, for up to 1 day.

Jumbo jack-o'-lantern cookies

MAKES 9 TO 10 COOKIES

½ cup all-purpose flour

½ cup whole wheat flour or additional all-purpose flour

½ teaspoon baking powder

¼ teaspoon baking soda

¼ teaspoon salt

1¼ teaspoons ground cinnamon

¼ teaspoon ground allspice

4 tablespoons (½ stick) butter at room temperature

½ cup honey

¼ cup (packed) brown sugar

1 large egg

½ teaspoon vanilla extract

½ cup pumpkin or winter squash purée, canned or homemade (see Two-Way Winter Squash Purée, page 34)

1 cup quick-cooking oatmeal

½ cup sunflower seeds

½ cup currants

½ cup miniature chocolate chips

½ cup diced dried apricots

Currants, chocolate chips, and/or chocolate-covered candies, etc., for decoration

Great fun for kids! These cookies are loaded with goodies.

◆ Preheat oven to 350°F. Grease 2 large baking sheets.

◆ Combine the all-purpose flour, whole wheat flour, baking powder, baking soda, salt, cinnamon, and allspice in a medium bowl. Set aside. Cream the butter, honey, and brown sugar in the large bowl of an electric mixer. Beat in the egg, vanilla, and pumpkin purée. (The mixture may not be smooth.) Stir in the flour mixture. Add the oatmeal, sunflower seeds, currants, chocolate chips, and apricots.

◆ Using a ⅓-cup measure, scoop the dough onto the baking sheets. With a rubber spatula, form the dough into a 5-inch-wide pumpkin shape with a little dough on the top for a stem. Repeat with the remaining dough. Decorate with currants, chocolate chips, etc. Bake for about 20 minutes, or until firm. Cool for 5 minutes on the pans, then transfer the cookies to a rack and cool completely.

Pumpkin-hazelnut cake with cream cheese frosting

The fruit purée or applesauce replaces most of the fat in this lightened pumpkin cake. The fruit and pumpkin purées both help improve the keeping qualities of the cake. You can substitute applesauce for the Lighter Bake.

MAKES 8 TO 10 SERVINGS

2 large eggs

⅓ cup Lighter Bake (apple and prune purée)

2 tablespoons vegetable oil

1 teaspoon vanilla extract

1½ cups all-purpose flour

1½ cups sugar

1 teaspoon baking soda

¼ teaspoon salt

1 teaspoon ground cinnamon

¼ teaspoon ground cloves

⅛ teaspoon ground nutmeg

1 cup pumpkin or winter squash purée, canned or homemade (see Two-Way Winter Squash Purée, page 34)

½ cup chopped hazelnuts

Cream Cheese Frosting (see method)

¼ cup sliced hazelnuts

CREAM CHEESE FROSTING

Makes about ¼ cup

4 ounces cream cheese at room temperature

½ teaspoon vanilla extract

1½ cups confectioners' sugar

◆ Preheat oven to 350°F. Combine the eggs, Lighter Bake, oil, and vanilla in a large bowl and mix well. In a medium bowl, stir together the flour, sugar, baking soda, salt, cinnamon, cloves, and nutmeg. Add to the egg mixture and beat well. Stir in the pumpkin purée and chopped hazelnuts. Pour into a greased 9-by-1½-inch round cake pan. Bake for 40 to 45 minutes, or until a wooden toothpick inserted near the center comes out clean. Cool for 5 minutes on a rack. Loosen edges and transfer to a serving plate.

◆ Frost the top and sides of the cake with Cream Cheese Frosting (see below) and garnish with sliced hazelnuts.

◆ To make the frosting: In a medium bowl, combine the cream cheese and vanilla, and sift in the confectioners' sugar.

◆ Cut into wedges to serve.

Swirled pumpkin cheesecake squares

Gingersnaps add pizazz to this rich-tasting dessert. Just a little bite is enough.

MAKES 16 PIECES

GINGERSNAP CRUST

About 20 gingersnaps, broken into large pieces

¼ cup granulated sugar

3 tablespoons butter, melted

CHEESECAKE FILLING

11 ounces (8- and 3-ounce packages) low-fat cream cheese at room temperature

⅓ cup low-fat sour cream

⅓ cup granulated sugar

1 tablespoon all-purpose flour

1 large egg

½ teaspoon vanilla extract

½ cup pumpkin or winter squash purée, canned or homemade (see Two-Way Winter Squash Purée, page 34)

1 tablespoon (packed) brown sugar

◆ Preheat oven to 325°F. Line the bottom and sides of a 9-by-9-by-2-inch square pan with foil. Grease the foil on the bottom and 1 inch up the sides of the pan.

◆ To make the crust: Process the gingersnaps in a food processor or blender until very finely chopped. You should have 1 cup of crumbs. Combine the gingersnap crumbs, sugar, and butter in a small bowl. Pat into an even layer in the bottom of the pan. Bake for 7 minutes. Cool on a rack.

◆ To make the filling: Beat the cream cheese, sour cream, granulated sugar, and flour in the large bowl of an electric mixer. Add the egg and vanilla and beat until smooth. Scoop ¾ cup of the cream cheese mixture into a medium bowl and stir in the pumpkin purée and brown sugar.

◆ Spoon the plain cream cheese mixture evenly over the crumb layer in the pan. Dollop the pumpkin mixture on top and swirl with a fork to make a decorative design. Bake for 25 minutes, or until firm in the middle when gently shaken. Cool in the pan for 1 hour. Chill thoroughly.

◆ To serve, lift cheesecake and foil from the pan. Cut into squares and remove from the foil to a serving plate.

Rum-raisin zucchini cake

MAKES ABOUT 10 SERVINGS

CAKE

½ cup dark and/or golden raisins

1 tablespoon rum

1½ cups all-purpose flour

1 teaspoon baking powder

¼ teaspoon baking soda

¼ teaspoon salt

1 teaspoon ground cinnamon

½ teaspoon ground ginger

¼ teaspoon ground nutmeg

6 tablespoons (¾ stick) butter, softened

½ cup granulated sugar

½ cup (packed) light brown sugar

1 large egg, beaten

1½ cups coarsely grated zucchini or other summer squash

RUM GLAZE

1 cup sifted confectioners' sugar

2 tablespoons rum, or 2 tablespoons milk plus ¼ teaspoon vanilla extract

Shredded zucchini lends a pretty green touch, but any summer squash can be used.

◆ Preheat oven to 325°F. Grease the bottom of 9-by-5-by-3-inch glass loaf pan. Line the bottom with wax paper.

◆ To make the cake: Combine the raisins and rum in a small bowl. Let stand, stirring occasionally. Meanwhile, in another small bowl, combine the flour, baking powder, baking soda, salt, cinnamon, ginger, and nutmeg. Set aside. Beat the butter, granulated sugar, and brown sugar in the large bowl of an electric mixer until well mixed. Add the egg and beat until creamy. Stir in the zucchini and the raisin and rum mixture. (The mixture may look curdled.) Gradually add the flour mixture and beat on low speed. Spoon the batter into the pan.

◆ Bake for 60 to 65 minutes, or until a wooden toothpick inserted in the center comes out clean. Cool for 10 minutes on a rack. Unmold and remove the wax paper. Cool completely.

◆ To make the glaze: Combine the confectioners' sugar and rum in a small bowl. Beat until smooth. Stir in a little warm water until a drizzling consistency is reached. Drizzle the glaze over the cooled cake. Let stand until the glaze hardens.

◆ Cut into ¾-inch slices to serve.

Pumpkin indian pudding

A Boston specialty, with a nod to my New England ancestors.

MAKES 4 SERVINGS

- 2 cups whole or skim milk
- 1/3 cup yellow cornmeal, preferably stone-ground
- 2 tablespoons butter, cut into small pieces
- 1/4 cup (packed) dark brown sugar
- 1/4 teaspoon ground cinnamon
- 1/4 teaspoon ground ginger
- Dash of ground nutmeg
- 1/8 teaspoon salt
- 1/2 cup pumpkin or winter squash purée, canned or homemade (see Two-Way Winter Squash Purée, page 34)
- 1 tablespoon molasses
- Vanilla ice cream to serve (optional)

◆ Preheat oven to 275°F. Butter a 1-quart baking dish.

◆ Combine the milk and cornmeal in a large heavy saucepan. Cook and stir over medium heat until the mixture is creamy, about 7 to 10 minutes. Remove from the heat. Add the butter and stir until melted. Combine the brown sugar, cinnamon, ginger, nutmeg, and salt in a small bowl. Stir into the milk mixture. Add the pumpkin purée and molasses. Pour into the dish. Bake for 1½ hours, or until a knife inserted near the center comes out clean.

◆ Serve warm with vanilla ice cream, if desired.

Glossary

Summer Squash

CROOKNECK AND YELLOW STRAIGHTNECK

Dark to pale yellow, smooth to bumpy skin. Crookneck, an old-fashioned squash, has a curved neck. Straightneck was developed for easy packing and shipping. Both are mild and delicately sweet, and can be used interchangeably. Yellow straightneck is lighter in color and fatter than yellow zucchini. Available most of the year.

PATTYPAN (SCALLOP, CYMLING)

Pale green and flavorful when young, becomes white and soft inside as it gets larger. Scalloped disk shape. Sunburst is a bright yellow hybrid with a ruffled edge and buttery taste. Scallopini, dark green with a flying saucer shape, is a cross between pattypan and zucchini. Peak season is July through September.

ZUCCHINI (ITALIAN SQUASH, COURGETTE)

Light to dark green to almost black, solid or striped, with a smooth skin. Gold Rush is a bright yellow, zucchini-shaped hybrid. The small green Ronde de Nice is a French heirloom zucchini, a round, firm fruit, creamy and fairly sweet. The original green varieties are available year-round.

Winter Squash

ACORN (TABLE QUEEN, DANISH)

Green to almost black, gold, or white-skinned squash, shaped like a deeply ridged acorn. Weighs 1 to 3 pounds. Hard rind with smooth texture. Mildly sweet, sometimes bland and fibrous. Green may be the most flavorful. Available year-round.

AUSTRALIAN BLUE (QUEENSLAND BLUE)

Pale blue, gray, or green skin, turns tan as it matures. A medium-large squatty pumpkin shape with deep ridges. Hard rind with sweet, bright orange meat. Keeps well.

BANANA

Originated in Mexico. Pale orange to pinkish white, shaped like a 3- to 4-foot-long banana. Soft rind with fine-textured, slightly sweet meat. Widely available. Frequently sold in 1- to 1½-pound chunks. Smaller blue and gray varieties, such as Banana Blue, are good quality and keep well.

BUTTERCUP

Dark green with a gray-green "turban" on the blossom end, shaped like a flattened drum. Weighs 3 to 5 pounds. Soft rind with a yellow-orange meat that may be dry. Very sweet, nutlike flavor.

BUTTERNUT

A group of squashes with smooth, beige skin, generally cylindrical in shape with a round bulge at the blossom end. Weighs 2 to 5 pounds. Thick, dark golden meat with small seed cavity. Soft rind with mild texture. Nutty-sweet flavor. Widely available year-round.

CALABAZA (WEST INDIAN PUMPKIN)

Generic name for several large round or pear-shaped squashes found throughout the Caribbean and Central and South America. Can be green with yellow stripes, tan, or orange. Hard rind with fine-grained, yellow-orange meat. Mild flavor. Available year-round in some Latin American markets. Often sold in precut chunks.

CARNIVAL

Recent cross between acorn and Sweet Dumpling. Colorful horizontal and vertical orange, green, yellow, and cream-colored stripes. About the same size as an acorn squash, but a rounder shape. Deep yellow, fibrous meat with large seed cavity. Sweet, earthy flavor.

DELICATA (SWEET POTATO SQUASH)

Lengthwise green stripes over an ivory base; skin turns orange as it ripens. Elongated in shape. Weighs 1½ to 2 pounds. Soft rind with yellow-gold meat and creamy texture. Slightly sweet, delicate flavor.

GOLD NUGGET (GOLDEN NUGGET)

Orange skin, often with a green ring around the stem, shaped like a miniature Cinderella coach. Very hard, inedible rind, grooved like a small pumpkin. Smooth, bright orange meat. Sweet and moist, but bland if picked immature. Because of the hard shell, it is best to cook whole, either by microwaving or baking.

HUBBARD (GOLDEN, BLUE, GREEN WARTED, OR BABY BLUE)

A group of squashes with tapered ends like spinning tops. Green, orange, tan, or blue-gray, either smooth or warty. Most are large, 8 to 12 pounds or more, but some varieties, like Baby Blue, are small. Hard rind with sweet, golden meat. Rich and creamy. Difficult to cut. Keeps well. Available year-round, often sold in large pieces.

KABOCHA (JAPANESE PUMPKIN)

A group of Hokkaido-type squashes popular in Japan. Green or gray uneven stripes or bright orange skin, flattened round shape. Soft rind with orange meat. Rich flavor. Available most of the year.

LARGE FIELD PUMPKIN

Orange skin, oval or round. Can weigh over 100 pounds. Soft rind good for carving. Orange meat often stringy. Some varieties good for cooking; most are watery with poor flavor. Generally best for jack-o'-lanterns or as serving dishes. Hard to find after Halloween. Perishable.

MINI-PUMPKIN (JACK-BE-LITTLE, MUNCHKIN)

Orange skin, brings to mind a tiny jack-o'-lantern. Often used as a decoration. Small, between 4 and 16 ounces. Orange meat with large seed cavity. Mildly sweet. Good size for individual serving, ideal for stuffing.

PUMPKIN (SUGAR PUMPKIN, SUGAR PIE, NEW ENGLAND PIE PUMPKIN, BABY BEAR, TRIPLE TREAT)

Orange skin, oval or round. Small pie or cooking pumpkins average 5 to 6 pounds. Soft rind with thick, dense, non-stringy meat. Sweet flavor. Some varieties, such as Baby Bear, Lady Godiva, and Triple Treat, have hull-less seeds. Lumina and other white varieties are good for cooking and carving. Hard to find after Thanksgiving. Fairly perishable.

ROUGE VIF D'ETAMPES (ROUGE D'TAMPES, CINDERELLA, FRENCH PUMPKIN)

Heirloom French variety. Bright red-orange color, large, deeply lobed, slightly flattened pumpkin shape. Soft rind with dense meat. Flavorful, sweet, and nutty. Ideal as an edible serving dish.

SPAGHETTI SQUASH (VEGETABLE SQUASH, ORANGETTI)

Yellow watermelon-shaped squash. Developed in Japan. Weighs 2 to 4 pounds. Pale yellow meat separates into strands resembling spaghetti when cooked. Hard rind with mild, nutlike flavor. Not interchangeable with other winter squash. Available year-round.

SUGAR LOAF

Dark green stripes over light tan background, cylindrical shape. Developed at the Oregon Agricultural Experiment Station. Related to Delicata. Soft rind with yellow, firm, medium-dry meat with large seed cavity. Rich, sweet flavor. Ideal for stuffing.

SWEET DUMPLING (ORIGINALLY CALLED VEGETABLE GOURD)

Green stripes over a cream background; skin turns deep orange over yellow as it matures. Scalloped pumpkin shape. Weighs 1 to 1½ pounds. Developed in Japan. Soft rind with pale yellow-orange meat. Smooth and sweet. Good size for stuffing. Does not store well.

TURBAN (TURK'S TURBAN)

Brightly colored, usually orange mottled with green and white. Fancifully shaped squash topped with decorative knobs. Soft rind with orange meat. Sweet and moist. Use first as a decoration, then bake it.

Year-Round Squash

CHAYOTE (MIRLITON, CHRISTOPHENE, VEGETABLE PEAR, XUXU)

Light to dark green, mostly smooth, but sometimes spiny, skin sometimes ridged lengthwise. Pear-shaped chayote (pronounced cha-OH-tay) is in the genus *Sechium*, a cousin to the Cucurbita clan. Grown in the tropics of Mexico and Central America, as well as Florida. Popular in Louisiana. Average weight is ¾ pound. Similar to summer squash, but requires longer cooking. The single, flat seed is edible. Mild taste, somewhere between a cucumber and zucchini. Generally available year-round.

Index

Table of equivalents

The exact equivalents in the following tables have been rounded for convenience.

LIQUID/DRY MEASURES

U.S.	METRIC
¼ teaspoon	1.25 milliliters
½ teaspoon	2.5 milliliters
1 teaspoon	5 milliliters
1 tablespoon (3 teaspoons)	15 milliliters
1 fluid ounce (2 tablespoons)	30 milliliters
¼ cup	60 milliliters
⅓ cup	80 milliliters
½ cup	120 milliliters
1 cup	240 milliliters
1 pint (2 cups)	480 milliliters
1 quart (4 cups, 32 ounces)	960 milliliters
1 gallon (4 quarts)	3.84 liters
1 ounce (by weight)	28 grams
1 pound	454 grams
2.2 pounds	1 kilogram

LENGTH

U.S.	METRIC
⅛ inch	3 millimeters
¼ inch	6 millimeters
½ inch	12 millimeters
1 inch	2.5 centimeters

OVEN TEMPERATURE

FAHRENHEIT	CELSIUS	GAS
250	120	½
275	140	1
300	150	2
325	160	3
350	180	4
375	190	5
400	200	6
425	220	7
450	230	8
475	240	9
500	260	10